FALMOUTH

THROUGH TIME

Michael Bradley

AMBERLEY PUBLISHING

Acknowledgements

I was born and grew up in Falmouth just after the Second World War. My old schools of Wellington Terrace Boys' School and the Falmouth Grammar School are still standing, although the school at Wellington Terrace is now an annexe of the University College Falmouth and the Grammar School is used for Adult Education classes. Both my old schools bring back so many fond memories and were so influential in my career. I left the town in the early 1960s to study Art and Art History and after an academic career in education I took early retirement following a serious heart condition. I returned to my home town in 1992 and was asked to join the Board of the Royal Cornwall Polytechnic Society based in Falmouth. It was there that I met Peter Gilson again, who was responsible for the Local History Archive at the RCPS, having taught me geography at the grammar school all those years ago. I am so grateful to Peter for all the knowledge he passed on to me and after he died in 2009 I was asked to continue the Archive which I am still involved with today.

There have been so many changes around the town, even in my lifetime, that it is difficult to record all of them, and I apologise for those I may have omitted. I hope this book shows some of the more important and memorable changes that have happened in recent times. I would like to thank all the people that helped in selecting photographs and researching text, including the team at the Local History and Research Group, Gerald Trethowan, 'Dinks' Banks, Alan and Ann Cox, Derek Asquith, Louis Turner, David Barnicoat, Peter Searle, Amanda Rundle, Katherine Hellings, and any others I may have omitted. I would also like to thank Thelma Gilson as well as the other members of the Board of the RCPS.

Finally I would like to thank my beautiful daughter, Hannah, for all her loving support and encouragement.

First published 2012

Amberley Publishing
The Hill, Stroud
Gloucestershire, GL5 4EP

www.amberley-books.com

Copyright © Michael Bradley, 2012

The right of Michael Bradley to be identified as the Author of this work has been asserted in accordance with the Copyrights, Designs and Patents Act 1988.

ISBN 978 1 84868 469 0

British Library Cataloguing in Publication Data. A catalogue record for this book is available from the British Library.

Typeset in 9.5pt on 12pt Celeste.
Typesetting by Amberley Publishing.
Printed in the UK.

Introduction

Situated on the south coast of Cornwall, the River Fal is one of the many examples of a drowned river valley known as a 'ria', formed when sea levels rose during the last warm inter-glacial period, many thousands of years ago. Its tidal creeks and deep water area, known as the Carrick Roads, beyond the estuary, form one of the finest natural harbours in the world. It has offered shelter to countless numbers of seafarers as well as being a centre for trade and commerce over several centuries.

The town of Falmouth just beyond the mouth of the river is not an old town when compared to others in the county, but offers a fascinating and rich history. Apart from Pendennis Castle and St Mawes Castle on either side of the estuary, both built by Henry VIII between 1539 and 1542, as well as the manorial home of Arwenack, there were just a few farms and fishermen's cottages. This can be clearly seen on the Burghley Map of 1595.

Arwenack, the ancestral home of the Killigrew family, was acquired in 1385 and remained in the family until well into the eighteenth century. With the protection of the two castles as well as the deep, sheltered harbour, the Killigrews saw the potential of building a town having been encouraged to do this when Sir Walter Raleigh stayed at Arwenack in 1596.

During the English Civil War, the Killigrews supported the Royalist cause and were generously rewarded for their loyalty. In 1660 they applied for the granting of a Royal Charter for the growing town, so that the settlement known as Smithick became the town of Falmouth for evermore. The town was already prospering both as a significant trading port as well as a centre for boat building owing to its favourable location, and by 1664 there were some 200 houses.

In 1688, the then government, through the Department of the Post Office established the Packet Service at Falmouth. Wars on the Continent had made travel extremely difficult so that mail and other precious cargoes were too vulnerable to send by road. The ships of the Packet Service were leased from private owners to act on behalf of the post office and initially carried diplomatic and commercial mail in 'pacquets' or parcels, hence its name. As well as commercial mail, gold and silver bullion were also carried and the service was extended to include assorted cargoes. Later, to add to the income of the ships' owners, passengers were also carried. The service initially served the Continent but with time this expanded to include North and South America as well as the Caribbean.

As a result, the Packet Service greatly contributed to the wealth of the town, with many people employed in servicing the ships. This included sail makers, rope makers, carpenters, fresh water suppliers, coopers and many other trades as well as ships' crews all contributing to the success of the service. However, with the invention of the steam engine, by 1830 the need for sailing ships declined. The situation became even worse and by 1851 the Packet Service came to a sad and final close at Falmouth.

At first the town keenly felt its loss, but through the far-sightedness of certain individuals, it began to recover when the Falmouth Docks Company was established in 1859. Shortly after, the Cornwall Railway built a branch line from Truro to the town in 1863, and thus a new industry was soon to develop.

Although Falmouth had been promoted as a health resort and within an area of outstanding natural scenery, it wasn't until the arrival of the railway that it could be fully developed as a tourist destination. The first commercial hotel on the seafront, the luxurious Falmouth Hotel, opened in 1865, soon to be followed by many others along the front that overlooked the magnificent Falmouth Bay. Guest houses and other establishments quickly sprung up within the town, to cater for the rapidly growing numbers of visitors. Pleasure boats, most of them built by Cox & Co., at Falmouth Docks, were soon operating from the various quays and piers within the harbour, to sail the beautiful tidal creeks of the River Fal and beyond.

Falmouth Docks grew as a world famous ship-repair centre and was recognised for its outstanding contribution through two world wars. Although the Docks have undergone several changes in its history, it continues to be innovative with the development of Pendennis Shipyard, a company that has established a worldwide reputation for both an excellent skilled workforce and a facility for building and developing luxury super-yachts. Future plans for the Docks include the ability to handle large, luxury cruise ships as well as a large yachting marina, evidence of the growing importance of the town as a yachting centre.

Other developments have taken place within the town's educational establishments, with the one-time Falmouth School of Art becoming the University College Falmouth, now recognised worldwide for its academic excellence.

Falmouth has seen many changes, which are included in this book, especially since the 1950s. Despite the changes, it continues to maintain its charm and individuality, offering an especially warm welcome to visitors to the town.

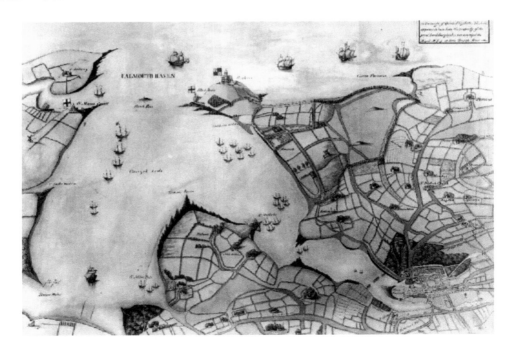

Engraving of Pendennis Castle, *c.* 1770

The imposing Pendennis Castle stands guard over the entrance to Falmouth harbour and the town beyond. Built by Henry VIII between 1539 and 1542 as well as St Mawes Castle, it was one of four originally planned, but only the two were built. The dry moat and hornworks seen in the engraving above were added at a later date by Queen Elizabeth I. Below, the headland, docks and town are clearly visible, with the white building of the Falmouth Hotel, centre left.

Arwenack Manor

Arwenack Manor can be seen above as it would have looked in the sixteenth century. It was the ancestral home of the famous Killigrew family but the house was destroyed by fire in 1646 following events in the English Civil War. It never regained its full glory after it was rebuilt and was occupied by several different people and organisations after the Killigrews had left. It was sadly neglected for many years and again was badly damaged by fire in the 1960s. However, after extensive research and with great building skill it was restored in 1979 to provide four private dwellings within the overall building.

Engraving of Falmouth Harbour, 1830

This scene of Falmouth harbour with Pendennis Castle in the far distance shows the town largely confined to the waterfront. The tower of the parish church is shown but beyond that it is open fields. On the left cattle are being driven down into the town from Bassett Street, to add to the rural feel of the scene. This was the only route into the town before the road along past the Greenbank was built in the early 1800s. Contrast that with today, below, showing Beacon Street with the Falmouth Docks in the distance and cars parked everywhere.

John Bull (1770–1851)

As commander of the packet ship, the *Duke of Marlborough*, John Bull was a colourful and forthright character. He built Marlborough House seen on the next page and lived there until his death in 1851, the year the Packet Service ended in Falmouth.

The superb painting of HM brig *Crane* by J. Condy, typical of a packet ship shows her entering Falmouth harbour with St Mawes Castle in the background. It is thought the painting was commissioned to commemorate the final arrival of a packet ship into the port. With the invention of the steam engine and the arrival of the railway, sailing vessels could no longer compete with the faster journey times, thus bringing to an end a golden age in the town's history.

Marlborough House, Built *c.* 1820

This beautifully proportioned mansion that overlooked Swanpool was built by John Bull, the famous Packet Service commander. Named after his ship, the *Duke of Marlborough*, he lived there with his second wife until his death in 1851. The fine building has many interesting features including rare French wallpaper from 1827 that can be seen in the drawing room. The lower view is of the house from the rear, with lawns in the grounds that reached down to the Swanpool.

Turnpike Creek

Turnpike Creek on the Penryn River, just north of the town, became the last resting place for many of the old coastal sailing boats no longer needed after the introduction of steam-driven vessels. In the background, Thomas's boatyard can be seen as well as several houseboats at low tide. The yachting marina below completely changed the whole character of the area with moorings for hundreds of luxury yachts and cruisers, as well as having a chandlery and restaurant.

The Tollhouse Opposite Turnpike Creek, 1950s

The Tollhouse or Turnpike known as 'The Falmouth Gate' was at the bottom of Old Hill and controlled the two main roads into Falmouth from Penryn. The original way into the town was by way of Old Hill through to Bassett Street, on to Beacon Street to meet up with the top of the High Street. Below shows the junction of the two roads with Old Hill in the centre and Marine Parade, built in the early 1800s, to the left. This road looks out over the Penryn River eventually to join up with the High Street, having passed Greenbank.

The Greenbank Hotel

The Greenbank Hotel dates back to when there was a simple alehouse on the site in 1670, and is the oldest hotel in Falmouth. The building above, built in 1785, was a stopping point for the mail coach service between Falmouth and Exeter. Commanding a fine view over Falmouth harbour, it was popular with passengers waiting to join their packet ships anchored in the King's Reach, off Trefusis. Today it is a major hotel and conference centre and within a short walk to the town centre via the High Street.

Dunstanville Terrace and the Greenbank

The large houses, many of them listed, were built at the beginning of the nineteenth century, to overlook the harbour and were occupied by many of the Packet Service ships' captains. The gentle pace of the horse-drawn busses and traps contrast with the motor cars of today. The children in the above photograph seem very willing to pose for the camera. In both, the Greenbank Hotel can be seen in the far distance.

Laundry Quay and Well Beach

Originally known as Pye's Cellars, Laundry Quay, situated near the top of the High Street, was a very busy part of the waterfront with two boat-building yards on either side of the quay. To the south was Thomas Jackett's Victoria Yard, with Thomas Gray's Well Yard to the north. The quay stood for many years until it was demolished to make way for a complex of luxury apartments seen below. Well Beach was reputedly the site for a series of smugglers' tunnels that led back under the road to the houses along the Greenbank.

The Royal Oak in Prince Street, *c.* 1910

Prince Street ran from the top of the High Street towards Greenbank and included several businesses including a dairy, a general store as well as the public house above. When compared with today it is difficult to imagine how busy this street was. The whole street was demolished as part of a clearance programme in the late 1950s, including Beacon Street that was above Prince Street. Eventually it was made into a public garden as seen below with wonderful views out over the harbour.

Prince Street at the Top of the High Street, _c._ 1880

The narrow Prince Street on the left connected the Greenbank and the High Street with Winchester Buildings on the right of the central block. The old chapel seen above was built in 1715 and enlarged in 1789. With the increasing volume of traffic in the 1930s, the central part was demolished to allow greater access especially for the Falmouth to Penryn buses. Prince Street was totally demolished in the late 1950s.

After the High Street Fire, April, 1862

One of the largest fires ever seen in Cornwall was that of Falmouth's High Street in the April of 1862. Fanned by strong winds it destroyed over thirty houses and dwellings, several businesses and left over 400 people homeless. When rebuilt, the road was widened by a further 10 feet under a compulsory purchase order. It is hard to imagine the High Street being 10 feet narrower than it is today!

High Street, Formerly Ludgate Hill, *c.* 1900

The busy street scene contrasts with that of today. Once known as Ludgate Hill, the High Street was the main access road into the town. Note the pawnbrokers on the left again with the children eager to have their photograph taken. The 'bridge' at the top of the High Street, seen below, was added when the complex of apartments were built on the left. The High Street now supports a variety of interesting, individual shops and restaurants to maintain its old world charm.

Two-Way Traffic in the High Street, Early 1960s

It is hard to imagine that traffic such as the Falmouth to Penryn buses used the High Street as part of their route. Buses even went in both directions, with pedestrians at risk with cars mounting the pavements! Today the narrowness is self evident when seen with the huge lorry coming down, below, and is now part of the one-way system for traffic movement in the town.

Barham's Bicycle Shop, Lower High Street, Early Twentieth Century

The photograph shows V. F. Barham as a young man outside his bicycle shop in the lower High Street. Many children in the town will have bought their first bicycle from these premises including the author, when it was continued by his son, Fisher Barham in the 1950s. The shop underwent several changes and today it is that of Stones Bakery, seen below, producing traditional, freshly-baked bread and pastries of exceptional quality on the premises.

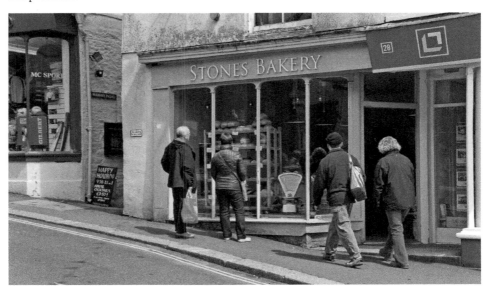

The Harbour, Docks and Town From Erisey Terrace, *c.* 1895

Taken by William Marsden Harrison a well known local photographer, the docks and harbour can be seen with Pendennis Castle in the far distance. To the right of Pendennis Point is the square building of the Falmouth Hotel on the seafront. Grose's General Drapery and Carpet Warehouse is seen in the centre of the photograph, and led into Market Street. Below today, the Prince of Wales Pier is seen, with the former Kings Hotel site, rebuilt in the 1980s, towering over the other buildings.

Market Strand Pier, *c.* 1895
Taken in the summer of around 1895, the pier then known as the Market Strand Pier, shows a busy scene with passengers waiting to board the many pleasure boats that operated from there. The vessel with the cross on her funnel was the *Emperor*. As a result of the growing demand for more landing space due to the increased number of pleasure boats, Market Strand Pier, opened in 1871, was extended and became the Prince of Wales Pier in 1905. Today the pier with its many boats and ferries, offers wonderful views out over the harbour.

Prince of Wales Pier, 1903

With the growth in tourism and the expansion of recreational boat trips, the Market Strand Pier became very congested. The solution was to expand out into the harbour and here HRH the Prince of Wales can be seen laying the foundation stone in 1903, escorted by Princess Mary of Teck. In the distance several of the large yachts are dressed with flags for the royal visit. The pier today is the focal point for most of the pleasure boats that ply the River Fal and beyond. The original foundation plaque is seen below.

The Entrance to the Prince of Wales Pier, *c.* 1910

The pier with its tool booth at the entrance to the extended section is seen above. Note the horse-cab rank in the centre, one of many around the town. The bay windows of Lake's, a local printers, are on the left. They published the local newspaper, the *Falmouth Packet*, which is still being printed today. On the right is the King's Hotel built in 1903. The site was rebuilt in the early 1980s with shops underneath and recently converted flats above. The cone-roofed booths below are for booking local boat trips mainly for the River Fal.

Harris's Coal Yard With Collier, 1930s

A steam crane of Harris's yard can be seen unloading a consignment of coal from the Grimsby collier moored alongside. In the distance are the two chimneys of the power station on The Beacon, with the rear of the High Street behind the coal depot. Below, the yard has been developed into several attractive waterside houses known as Mulberry Court. In the seventeenth century this area known as Mulberry Square was home to many of the town's merchants and businessmen.

Market Strand, *c.* 1895

This area of the town was originally the site of Smithick Creek, the focal point of the settlement that developed to become the Falmouth of today. The first market house opposite the creek was once a beach or 'strand', hence its name today. In the distance, the very narrow High Street can be seen. It was from the Strand that the last staging coach left Falmouth in 1863, having been replaced by the newly arrived railway. Below left is the former Kings Hotel that was built in 1903.

Market Strand, c. 1910

The photograph shows the newly built Kings Hotel with its parapet over the pavement. Next door is the retail shop of the Redruth Brewery Company and Eastman's, a butcher shop, next door again. The photograph below shows the entrance into Market Street with the large granite building formerly the Capital and Counties Bank and the Café Royal above. The site of the Kings Hotel on the left now has several retail shops.

Carnes Brewery Depot, Market Street, c.1900
Workers take time to pose outside the W. E. Carnes Brewery depot at 44, Market Street. This was replaced by the first Marks & Spencer's store in Cornwall in 1937. The store expanded to include the Provincial Bank next door, with its granite façade that can still be seen today, below. The Carnes Brewery was between Webber Street and lower Killigrew Street and is now a well-known supermarket.

Bell's Court, off Market Street

Hidden away behind the main street, this was the original offices for the Packet Service agents and where the reading of the Riot Act took place in 1810. As a result, the Packet Service moved to Plymouth, but due to impracticable circumstances it returned to Falmouth in February 1811. The court was named after George Bell who was the agent there between 1747 and 1776.

Today, following use as the Falmouth Maritime Museum and later as the Cornwall Maritime Museum, before the National Maritime Museum Cornwall was opened, it has been restored and is now a tasteful delicatessen and restaurant.

County Police Station, Market Street, 1900

Following the enormous fire in Market Street in 1870, the county police station was miraculously saved and is seen above, with its retaining cells below street level. It was eventually closed when the police service was transferred to the new larger building in Berkeley Avenue in 1901. The contrast with today is very apparent having been converted into a shop that has changed its usage several times. The original police cells are said to still exist.

The Royal Hotel, Market Street, 1960s

The Royal Hotel was one of the oldest in Falmouth having been built in 1789, before being replaced by the Midland Bank in 1967. Today it is the HSBC Bank with a gymnasium above. The ABC sign seen in the upper photograph shows the entrance to the cinema, previously the Grand Cinema, as well as the main entrance to the hotel. Looking into Market Street, the clock of W. H. Samuel, jeweller's, can be seen. The street is part of the one-way traffic system through the centre of the town and as yet has not been pedestrianised.

Smithick Hill also known as Back Hill, 1920s

The whole of this area was due for demolition in the 1930s under the local Slum Clearance programme, but was not finally achieved until the late 1950s. The upper photograph shows Smithick School at the far end of the row of cottages, with their drying poles for washing attached to the outside walls. One of the many basic corner shops can be seen but sadly no longer exists. Rollings bakery was on the left and is now a private house. The area is now overgrown and empty in comparison with earlier times.

Open Fish Market at Fish Strand Quay, c. 1900

At one time the fish market was next to the Royal Hotel in Market Street but this was moved to the quay in the late nineteenth century, after several complaints from hotel guests. Local fishmongers such as the Chard family were part of the waterfront scene as they bid for the freshly caught catch. Next to the market was an ice factory and storage facilities for the local fishermen. Today the market site has become the Waterman's Inn seen below.

Chard's Wet Fish Shop, Church Street, 1970s

After several generations of the Chard family fish selling business, it finally closed in the 1970s. The entrance tunnel to the former Gas Works can be seen on the left. This is now a car park with magnificent views over the harbour. The shop front above was restored by Mr Colin Nunn, to match his shop next door, where he sold maps and old prints. The fish shop is now a coffee shop, de Wynn's, named after James Wynn who built the first gas works behind the main street. Falmouth became the first town in Cornwall to be lit by gas in 1819.

Snow's Court, c. 1910

Leading off Church Street, the steep, cobbled passage housed several families and small workshops. In 1912 this was demolished and rebuilt by the Harris brothers, local entrepreneurs, to become the St Georges Cinema. It was considered one of the finest in the county and seated over a thousand people. The cinema, badly damaged by fire in the 1950s, was reopened in the early 1960s as a shopping arcade and coffee shop. The St Georges Arcade still retains its original façade.

Church Street, c. 1880

The centre of Falmouth, with the waterfront to the rear, consists of shops, galleries and restaurants and is still very narrow as seen in both photographs. The Subscription Rooms above, with the six columns, were built in 1826 and was in effect a 'gentlemen's club'. It was converted into two shops in the 1920s and the flat above added at a later date. At the far end of Church Street is the parish church of King Charles the Martyr, built in 1662.

Upton Slip and the Bosun's Locker

Leading off Church Street, Upton Slip is one of the many 'opes' or passageways that led to the waterfront. These gave access to the many trading premises and small workshops leading from them. On the right can be seen the Bosun's Locker, once a sail loft, but now a yachting chandlers. Opposite is the sail makers, Penrose's, established in 1826. The large unknown ship's figurehead has been a fixture at Upton Slip for many years.

Below, the sail loft of Prior and Holdruff was typical of the many sail makers that worked along the town's waterfront, during the golden age of sail. It was situated where the Bosun's Locker is today. The 'ope' was named after James Upton, mayor of Falmouth in 1708.

Church Street Looking North, *c.* 1890s

The busy street scene shows shoppers as well as postmen outside what was then the main Post Office. Interestingly there is no form of transport in the photograph, not even a horse and cart! On the right is Sander's Temperance Hotel and the Cornwall Bank (with the railings), next to it. The Royal Cornwall Polytechnic Society founded in 1833 is opposite on the left. The temperance hotel is now a retail outlet selling pasties, with private accommodation above.

Peter's Bakery Shop, Church Street, c. 1900

Peter's bakery shop was very popular in the town with its tempting window display of cakes and pastries freshly baked at the rear of the premises. Family members stand outside the shop, one with a large basket to run errands for the bakery. The shop later became a jewellery business run by Mr Hansel Beechey-Newman in the 1960s. The original shop frontage has survived today and is now a hair salon, giving this part of the town an old world charm.

King Charles the Martyr Church and Cemetery, 1950s

Following the restoration of the monarchy in 1660, the church was built in 1662 to the memory of King Charles I and named after him. Before 1964, the cemetery divided New Street from Porhan Street but following the building of the road below, to run behind the main street of the town, Porhan Street was closed and the name dropped for ever, so it all became New Street. Sadly the road was never completed beyond Well Lane.

Church Corner Horse – Taxi Rank, *c.* 1895

The top photograph shows one of the many horse-taxi ranks in the town, with Aaron Smith (centre left) the proprietor of the taxi business opposite, where the children are standing. The King's Head Hotel is open with Mr Ladbrooke and his family posing on the doorstep. Children of that time seem fascinated with photography and are willing to stand before the camera! Today, the whole of the main street is a busy one-way system with cars parked in front of the King Charles the Martyr church.

Two-Way Traffic in Arwenack Street, 1940s

It is difficult to believe that two-way traffic was allowed through the centre of the town but the photograph shows a lone policeman struggling to deal with a snarl up, in the late 1940s. The narrowness of the main street can be better seen below where traffic is now one-way. Many of the buildings in this street are listed and at one time were residential before the development of shops on the ground floor.

Arwenack Street Looking North, *c.* 1885

The busy street scene above is at the junction with Swanpool Street. The shipping chandlery of Mr Vos is on the corner of Swanpool Street with a horse and cart passing by. The photograph shows several carts coming through the street long before motor cars became popular. Today the street is busy with several good restaurants and shops and is once again. one-way The front of the Quayside Inn is on the right, with the rear of the premises overlooking Custom House Quay.

Regina Unloading Road Stone at Custom House Quay, 1930s

Road stone was brought from the quarries on the Lizard, south of Falmouth and used to maintain and build new roads around the town. Piles of stone can be seen outside the Harbourmaster's Office, from the *Regina* with the boat being the most economical means of transporting this type of material. The name of the Globe Hotel has changed to the Quayside Inn and cars are now allowed to park on the quay. Many of the small boats are privately owned and are permanently moored in the basin.

Entrance to Custom House Quay, 1950s

Compared with the lower photograph the quays seem much quieter and less cluttered than with today. Above, a steam tug can be seen near the Docks, with Trefusis Point behind. The large floating dock next to the ship is also shown. Below the red brick structure, known as The King's Pipe, is to the rear of the Custom House. It was used to burn confiscated tobacco and other goods seized by the customs men in the past. Next to this is a granite drinking fountain placed there in 1830.

Grove Place, *c.* 1900

Part of the Killigrew Estate at Arwenack was sold in the 1830s and the land used to develop the fine houses seen in Grove Place, above. Bank House, to the right of the terrace of houses, was built by the Fox family in 1788 and is now converted to luxury apartments. The beach below the seawall was used at low tide by boats to work on repairs and clean below the waterline. However, it was filled in the 1920s with spoil from excavation work at Falmouth Docks, and is now a car park.

The Killigrew Monument and Grove Place, c. 1895
This part of the town was known as the Bank and has undergone considerable change in the last eighty years. Above, the railway track from the Royal Engineers Barracks nearby is seen leading onto Submarine Pier, built in 1892. Further infilling of land that was once a beach opposite Grove Place, near the Killigrew Monument, today serves as a car park for the shops and restaurants in Events Square as well as the National Maritime Museum Cornwall.

The Grove, c. 1830

Following the sale of part of the Killigrew Estate, the Killigrew Monument was dismantled from its original location within a grove of elm trees. It was moved piece by piece to a new location further south but still kept within the estate. This 'primitive' painting by an unknown artist shows the dismantling prior to the move. The elegant row of houses, below, were then built on the site to give outstanding views over the harbour. Today they are mostly small hotels or restaurants that overlook Events Square.

The Killigrew Monument With Falmouth Docks

Photographed in the 1960s, Submarine Pier and Falmouth Docks can be seen to the left of the Killigrew Monument, with Trefusis Point beyond. The monument was again relocated in 1871 following the arrival of the railway and the building of houses in what is now Lansdowne Road. Today it stands opposite Arwenack Manor; a fitting tribute to the Killigrew family that once lived there. With the development of Events Square, seen below, sadly the wonderful open view has been lost.

The Bar in Snow

This very unusual photograph of part of the town known as The Bar was taken in the harsh winter of 1962 and shows several barges tied up at the Submarine Pier with Pendennis Point in the distance. The pier, built in 1892 was connected to the Royal Engineers barracks nearby, by a single narrow gauge railway line. The area has been completely redeveloped with the sheds behind the pier now gone. In its place the National Maritime Museum Cornwall has been built, below.

The Tide Mill and Timber Pond, c. 1900

The Tide Mill, to the right of the ship with the sail, was built by Peter Killigrew in 1675 and remained until it was finally demolished in 1914. The timber pond, above, was used to season wood prior to its use for boat-building in the boatyards nearby. Below, taken from a similar viewpoint, the National Maritime Museum Cornwall was opened by HRH The Queen in 2003. Next to it stands a small boat marina, with the town in the distance. The observation tower at the NMM offers wonderful views over the harbour and docks.

The RE Barracks, Bar Road

The curved roof of the barracks was a well known landmark in this part of the town and served many purposes in its time, including a dance hall. Originally the whole complex was built for the Submarine Miners, Royal Engineers in 1892 and later became the headquarters for the military training of part-time soldiers. It was demolished in 2005 with a new hotel proposed for the site. Instead it has become a car park for the National Maritime Museum Cornwall at Events Square, nearby. Bar Road can be seen in the distance.

The Royal Yacht *Britannia*, 1977

The Royal Yacht *Britannia* can be seen making her way to the County Wharf on one of her many visits to the port. This occasion was for the Queen's Silver Jubilee Tour of 1977. In the background are the Submarine Pier and the curved roof of the Royal Engineers Barracks in Bar Road. The Submarine Pier was dismantled in 1985 and soon after, in 1988, work started on laying the foundations for Port Pendennis, a yachting and residential complex.

The Docks Estate, c. 1865

This very early view of the newly founded Falmouth Docks Company (1860) shows the early development around the first two graving or dry docks, with the Eastern Breakwater beyond. In No. 2 Graving Dock is a steam ship, her funnel just visible, with a sailing vessel to its stern. Below, the Queen Elizabeth II Dry Dock, on the left stands empty awaiting its next large ship. The enormous crane overshadows the Pendennis Shipyard complex where world-class superyachts are designed, built and maintained.

The No. 2 Dry Dock at Falmouth Docks

The early image, taken in around 1890, by William Marsden Harrison shows two sailing ships in the No. 2 Dry Dock as well as a steam vessel in the No. 1 Dry Dock next to them. Other ships are moored alongside the Eastern Breakwater. Note the wooden beams extending from the walls of the dry dock to support the ships and keep them upright. Below, a cross-channel ferry nearly fills the Queen Elizabeth II Dry Dock, formerly No. 2 Dock, awaiting a refit. The photograph was taken from the Castle Drive, which gives a magnificent view over the Docks.

The Fish Landing Beach Inside the Docks, *c.* 1890

Several fishing fleets from all over the country came to the port to land their catch. Above, the fleet from Lowestoft can be seen in the distance, with the large white sailing ship at anchor. On the beach, teams of men work to load the carts with baskets and barrels of freshly caught fish. This was then sent to London by rail for export to many of the Mediterranean countries. As the fishing industry went into decline the beach was replaced by a further two dry docks, as seen in the aerial view below.

The Bombing of Falmouth Docks, July 1940

Although photography was restricted during the Second World War, especially of military installations, the bombing of Falmouth Docks was captured on film from along the Greenbank. Three ships were severely damaged, including the BP tanker the *British Chancellor*, and six men were killed as a result of the enemy assault. The aerial view, seen below, shows the Docks in the early 1950s. Slowly the country was beginning to recover from the Second World War and Falmouth Docks became extremely busy. Over fifteen ships can be counted, with many in the port for a refit and others for major repairs. The skill of the local workforce was such that Falmouth Docks established a reputation as one of the finest repair yards in the whole of Europe.

The *Pamir* Alongside the County Wharf, 1956

The German sailing ship visited the town for the last time in 1956. Sadly she was sunk in the South Atlantic Hurricane Carrie of 1957, with eighty seamen lost. There were only six survivors from her crew. Built in 1905 she made many voyages, particularly carrying nitrates from all over the world. Below the luxury cruise ship the *Balmoral* is on the County Wharf on her first visit to the port in 2010.

The Harbour From Above the Bar

This early photograph of around 1875 was taken above the railway station, looking out over the harbour. There are several boatbuilding yards shown, including those of Lean's and Trethowan's. On the right is the foundry of Cox & Company one of the first engineering works in the Docks. Below the Docks, on the right, are the buildings of Port Pendennis, and the National Maritime Museum Cornwall is seen on the left. In the distance the town makes a perfect backdrop to the harbour.

Falmouth Railway Station, c. 1898

The railway from Truro took four years to build, finally arriving in Falmouth in 1863. Above, the wide roof of the station can be seen with a train carriage beneath. The two children seem very amused, unaware of the pony and trap leaving the station, having possibly dropped off his passengers. Below, all that is left of the station site today, including the large block of flats built for student accommodation, that tower over the car park and the solitary, covered, railway platform.

Outside Falmouth Station, Easter Monday, 1904

The motor car seen above was the first to leave from the station on Easter Monday, 1904. The station, with its advertising hoarding, can be seen in the background as well as the large crowd gathered around the car. It is interesting to guess how comfortable a journey would have been, given the tyres used then! Below, the railway station as it was in the 1950s is seen, with parts of the town in the distance. Note the train under the platform roof as well as the large goods depot on the left.

The Falmouth Hotel and Seafront, *c.* 1880
Built and opened in 1865, the Falmouth Hotel stands alone with the Gyllyngdune Estate far off in the distant trees. A footpath went along the whole of the seafront above the beaches and rocks, with the section in front of the hotel known as the Invalids' Walk. A road was eventually built the entire length of the seafront, with the final section linking up with Castle Drive in 1908. Today several first-class hotels are built along the seafront to overlook the Falmouth Bay.

Cliff Road on the Seafront

The coastguard cottages are clearly seen in the upper photograph along with the water tower and garrison houses, built in 1902. This was the final section of the seafront completed in 1908 and joined with Castle Drive around the Pendennis Point. Today considerable housing 'infill' and development have obscured the cottages, with luxury apartments now built at the far end of the row. The 'Ships and Castles' swimming pool complex is seen on the skyline. Note all the cars along the seafront.

Swanpool Looking South, *c.* 1890

The Swanpool and beyond to Swanpool Beach has always been a popular walk for visitors and townspeople alike. The very open scene above shows Swanpool, the unmade road and lack of any traffic giving it a rural, peaceful feel. In fact it is a short walk to the town, with several houses now built around the pool. Today Swanpool has developed somewhat. Hedgerows and rushes have grown around its edge to become a nature reserve and conservation area as well as a Site of Special Scientific Interest.

The Bay Hotel

This elegant hotel, built in 1908, was owned by the same consortium that owned the Falmouth Hotel further along the seafront. The beautiful interior of bevelled glass and rich panelling added to its splendid ambience and atmosphere. On the seafront opposite, the hotel even had its own access to the beaches below by way of a viewing platform and steps. Sadly the hotel was demolished in 1993 and developed into the block of luxury flats known as Bay Court, seen below.

The Opening of the Bandstand, Gyllyngdune Gardens

Gyllyngdune Gardens were opened in 1907 by the local MP's wife, Mrs Mary Goldman. The marquee seen behind the bandstand was a temporary measure until the completion of the Princess Pavilion Theatre, which was opened in 1911 by HRH Princess Alexander of Teck. Today the listed bandstand and surrounding walkways have been totally restored to complement the outstanding work of Falmouth Town Council. The fernery, shell grotto and former tea rooms have been transformed into a delightful venue for those wanting to relax and enjoy the peaceful surroundings.

Gyllyngdune Gardens, c. 1910

The gardens, originally called the Winter Gardens, were opened in 1907. There was access from the seafront and the gardens included a fernery, transformed from the remains of the quarry that had provided stone for many of the nearby buildings. A grotto decorated with shells was also incorporated into the gardens, as well as walkways that led to the greenhouses, seen above. The steps on the right led up to the bandstand and theatre previously mentioned. In 2011 all of the gardens were beautifully restored as can be seen below.

Gyllyngvase Beach *c.* 1890

Gyllyngvase Beach has always been a popular spot for both visitors and the local population, offering a fine, sandy beach and safe bathing. There were few hotels at this end of the seafront and scarcely any residential development, as seen above. The early beach café is shown, along with the strange looking platform on wheels used to land daytrippers onto the beach from visiting passenger boats. This contrasts with the crowded beach scene below, which includes a fine restaurant and hotels as well as the luxury apartments that overlook Falmouth Bay.

The Entrance to Gyllyngvase Beach, *c.* 1910

As tourism developed, more and more hotels were built, overlooking Falmouth Bay and offering magnificent views as far south as the Manacles. As the beaches grew in popularity, facilities such as the beach café, changing huts and even donkey rides were introduced. The old anchor seen above came from an old naval ship the *St. Vincent,* which had been dismantled in Falmouth Docks in 1906. The new 'Gylly Café' seen on the right, below, is always extremely busy and gives superb views out over the beach and the bay.

Queen Mary Gardens, 1912

The gardens were originally an area of marshy, foul-smelling ground just behind the beach at Gyllyngvase. As visitor numbers increased, it was decided to turn the ground into an attractive space for rest and relaxation. The land was drained and laid out with plants and shrubs with intersecting walkways, as seen above. The gardens were opened by Mrs. Mary Goldman in 1912. Today they are beautifully maintained by the Falmouth Town Council Parks Department and bring a wealth of colour to the scene. The Falmouth Beach Resort Hotel is seen in the background.

Haymaking in Fields Above the Seafront, *c.* 1890

Nowadays it is difficult to imagine this rural scene of haymaking in the fields above Gyllyngvase Beach. It shows the open nature of the seafront in the late nineteenth century, still largely undeveloped apart from Membly Hall in the distance. These same fields are now covered with large houses such as those of Boslowick Road. Below, the seafront, seen beyond Gyllyngvase Beach, now consists of luxury apartment blocks, which have replaced many of the hotels that were previously there.

The First Observatory, 1970s
Built by the Royal Cornwall
Polytechnic Society in 1867,
the observatory was one of
only seven in the whole of the
United Kingdom. Used for
meteorological observations,
it was closed after a larger
observatory was built on
Western Terrace in 1885, not
far from the recreation ground.
In 2011, the whole structure
was completely renovated and
redesigned internally, and the
camera obscura on the top floor
put back into working order.
This had been added originally
after the Second World War to
give wonderful views over the
town. The present owners have
furbished the interior to a very
high standard and it is now let
out for holiday accommodation.
The view below, taken from the
'new' observatory, shows the
town and the Penryn River with
the village of Flushing opposite.

Falmouth Docks From the First Observatory, 1950s

Looking out over the town towards Pendennis Point. The castle, the Submarine Pier, the harbour dredger on its moorings and the two floating dry docks in the shipyard can all be seen above. Much of the waste ground seen beyond the Submarine Pier has been developed into Port Pendennis, a private housing complex that was started in 1988. Below, the Kings and Empire Wharves have been removed; however, the National Maritime Museum Cornwall with its pontoon is seen to the right, in front of the row of houses.

The Second Observatory, Western Terrace, c. 1885

Photographed here by William Marsden Harrison, the second, larger observatory replaced the earlier building of 1867 and had far more sophisticated scientific equipment. By 1885, the number of meteorological stations across the country had been reduced to just four and Falmouth was one of those that were kept. Observations were sent to the main weather office at Kew in London. The observatory was in use right up until 1952. Today it has been converted into a very tasteful small hotel, with the original pillar of the wind vane still to be seen on its roof.

The Recreation Ground, Late Nineteenth Century

The recreation ground at the top of Killigrew Street opened in 1887 and soon proved to be very popular for sports meetings, especially rugby and cycling. The rare photograph above shows the line-up for a penny-farthing cycle race with a good crowd of spectators in the open grandstand behind them. Today the ground is the home of Falmouth Rugby Football Club, with its new clubhouse, below. At other times in the past part of the Recreation Ground has been used for travelling circuses and fairs.

Circus Elephants in Upper Killigrew Street, 1890s

A visit from the circus, often with a parade through the main streets, caused great excitement in the town. Here a team of elephants and camels, towing a band of musicians, are making their way up Killigrew Street to the recreation ground and the big tent. As a form of entertainment the circus still visits the town occasionally, but it has largely gone out of fashion and animals are rarely used anymore. Upper Killigrew Street today is seen below; it is much the same apart from the cars parked everywhere.

The Classical and Mathematical School, Killigrew Street

The classical building above was built in 1825 and became a day school, later becoming Falmouth Grammar School. It soon became too small for its purpose and a new grammar school was built in Quarter Mile Lane (now Tregenver Road), opening in 1915. This still stands today and is used as the town's Adult Education Centre. The classical building was demolished in the late 1950s to be replaced by the Falmouth Technical College, which now houses the Falmouth Marine School, seen below.

Horse Bus at Berkeley Mews

Even though the combustion engine had been invented, cars were still relatively new when the photograph above was taken and public transport still relied on the use of horses as a means of travel. In this leafy mews Simon Gay's horse bus can be seen loaded with passengers ready for an excursion. In the background the new police station can just be seen, thus dating this as after 1901. Today the scene, shown below, is hardly recognisable with the Argos store and the former police station, which is now used for private housing.

Berkeley Place, Above the Moor

In this photograph from around 1901 Berkeley Place mostly consists of three-storey residential dwellings. In the 1930s this row of houses was developed by the Cooperative Retail Society and completely changed the character of this part of the town. The raised, covered fountain made of Cornish granite, seen below in front of the restaurant, originally stood inside the old market on the Moor. The market was demolished to make way for the post office that opened in 1930.

Cross Row, Above the Moor

Situated above the Moor, this row of cottages were demolished in the 1930s and the whole character of the area changed from residential to the commercial as shops replaced them. The corner premises of Party Zone seen below were once the showrooms of H. Rider, a local garage and car dealer. The Indian restaurant still has the original windows made of metal in the art deco style of the period. On the far corner the old police station can just be seen; it is now divided into residential units.

The Packet Memorial, the Moor, 1898

Built to celebrate the huge contribution the Packet Service had given to the town of Falmouth, the 38-foot granite obelisk was unveiled in 1898 with much pomp and ceremony. The photograph above shows the crowds at the event with Cross Row clearly visible beyond. Killigrew Street on the left was largely residential, and the Catholic church is seen in the far-off distance. Today the monument has been integrated into a 'traffic island', seen below, with Berkeley Place behind.

Killigrew Street, *c.* 1896

In the distance the Catholic church built in 1869 is seen, with children posing for the camera in this old photograph of Killigrew Street. A horse and cart is making a delivery of what appears to be coal outside Thomas's shop on the left. Today, the lower part of the street is incorporated into the one-way traffic system, with vans and cars parked on either side. Many of the lower floors of the houses have been converted into small shops. It is interesting to see how much the trees have matured.

Sports Outing on the Moor, 1932

The open nature of the Moor can be seen as the four open buses full of supporters wait to have their photograph taken before their departure. In the background is Cross Row, a row of cottages that were demolished in the late 1930s. This greatly contrasts with today, as the upper Moor has become a crowded car park with shops and a restaurant in the distance. Double-decker buses offload their passengers to the right.

Building the Library and Municipal Buildings, 1894

The public library and municipal building were built in 1894, thanks to the generosity of the benefactor John Passmore Edwards, and opened two years later. During this time the market on the Moor in Market Place, with its stalls and canvas covers, carried on trading, as seen above. The granite façade of the building is shown below to the left and now houses the Falmouth Art Gallery on the first floor. The farmers' market is a regular feature on the Moor today.

Fun Fair on the Moor, *c.* 1905

Fun fairs were regularly held on the Moor on the open space known as Market Place in front of the market house. This carried on until the fairs were moved to the top part of the Moor in later years and then to the recreation ground at the top of Killigrew Street. Above, families are exploring the swings and colourful sideshows. In the background is the central Methodist church, built in 1876. Today, the Moor has been completely redesigned, with parts set aside for pedestrians and disabled parking.

The Methodist Chapel on the Moor

John Wesley, the famous Methodist preacher, paid his first visit to the town in 1745 and as a result of further visits the chapel seen above was built in 1791. This was replaced by a much grander building in 1876, which was badly damaged in the Second World War bombing raids of 1940 and 1941. It was restored to its former glory and reopened in 1956, as seen below. Jacob's Ladder, with its one hundred and eleven steps, is to the right of the church.

The Moor, c. 1901

The open space of the Moor is seen, with children playing in what appears to be snow. To the extreme left is the clock tower of the Board School with the library and market house in front. In the centre is the town hall, built in 1864, with the chimney of Carne's Brewery to its left. The market house was bought by the Harris brothers and demolished in 1929 to make way for the post office, seen below. On the right is the original location of the Packet Memorial, now a traffic island.

The Western National Bus Depot, Berkeley Avenue

The depot was used primarily for maintenance work for a fleet of local buses, but it also served as the terminal for the Royal Blue coaches that operated nationally. Local buses left here and went to the main post office on the Moor, where departure points were located. The whole complex above was sold off and demolished to make way for various shops, seen below. In the distance is the former Drill Hall, built in 1874, now converted into the Phoenix Cinema.

Kimberley Croft, Formerly Trevethan Farm, 1990s

It is difficult to imagine the old farm that stood above and was the birthplace of the author. The original farm dated back to at least 1595 according to the Burghley Map of that date. From the 1950s the building was 'modernised' and the old apple orchard that was in front of the farmhouse was left to overgrow. Occupying a prime site, not far from Kimberley Park and the centre of the town, it was sold and developed into ten townhouses, some of which are seen below.

Falmouth School of Art, 1902

Although Art and Science classes were held in the municipal buildings on the Moor in 1896, the first purpose-built Falmouth School of Art opened in 1902 in Arwenack Avenue, shown on the left. In 1951 the school moved to Kerris Vean in Woodlane to accommodate the growing numbers of students. Its courses were awarded degree status in 1964. The School of Art became the Falmouth College of Art and Design, rapidly expanding in the 1980s and '90s under the leadership of Professor Alan Livingstone. It now offered advanced degrees as well as courses in Media Studies, Radio Broadcasting and Television Production amongst others. The college has now become the University College Falmouth based at Tremough in Penryn and is recognised as one of the finest throughout the world for its academic excellence. The lower photograph shows part of the university campus today at Tremough.

Dracena Avenue Looking South, 1923

The newly completed road has a few people walking along the opened section but no motor cars are in sight. In the distance the grandstands of the recreation ground are visible above the few houses in Dracena Avenue with mostly open fields on the right. In contrast, today the road is one of the busiest into town with cars waiting at the traffic lights and people queuing at the bus stop. On the left is a car showroom and garage.

Kimberley Park

The park was laid out on land given for the benefit of the people of the town in 1877 by Sir John Wodehouse, the Earl of Kimberley, with the then Borough Council acting as Trustee. With more and more land being used for housing development it was felt that a 'green space' was needed for rest and relaxation. The boating pool, seen above in the late 1940s, was very popular with the local children. Sadly this was filled in and grassed over in the 1990s so that only the steps that led down to the pool are still visible.

Kimberley Park, 1880

Children can be seen pushing their siblings in prams and homemade carts along one of the several paths that led around the park. On the left, behind the two seated figures, there was a fishpond. Park Terrace is just visible through the trees in the distance. The seated figure wearing the bowler hat seems to be resting his arm on some form of early camera. Below, the war memorial was moved from its original location on the seafront.

Building Work on Dracena Avenue, 1921

Work started on the 'new' road, to the rear of the town through the fields of Ashfield and Penwerris farms. The deep cutting seen above was once part of the town's golf course. It was made by teams of men using shovels as well as horses and carts. The work was contracted out to the local firm of E. Thomas & Co., and the road finally opened in 1923. Today, fast-moving traffic makes this the principal road into the town, with the Four Winds Inn on the left hidden behind the fir trees.

Dracena Avenue, 1923

To cater for the increased volume of houses to the rear of the town, the road above was built in 1923 and opened by Mr John Harris, the mayor of Falmouth. Stephen's Ropeworks can be seen above on the left, with its tall chimney and ropewalk. The open fields of Penwerris Farm are on the right with the wide road leading from Ashfield through to meet the recreation ground near the top of Killigrew Street. Today it has become the main route into the town.

The Seafront From Pendennis Point

The photograph above was taken by W. M. Harrison between 1898 and 1902. Seen from the castle ramparts, it shows the early development of the seafront with the building of many new hotels. Below, the town is seen from the same viewpoint and shows the spread of the town today. In conclusion, I would like to apologise for any omissions in this book. With so many changes it has been a difficult task but I hope I have succeeded in giving the reader a glimpse of *Falmouth Through Time*.